sustainable ENERGY

HOW CAN WE SAVE OUR WORLD?

sustainable
ENERGY

Angela Royston

ARCTURUS

This edition first published by Arcturus Publishing
Distributed by Black Rabbit Books
123 South Broad Street
Mankato
Minnesota MN 56001

Printed in the United States

Series concept: Alex Woolf
Editor and picture researcher: Patience Coster
Designer: Phipps Design
Consultant: Howard Sharman, University College London

Library of Congress Cataloging-in-Publication Data

Royston, Angela.
  Sustainable energy sources / Angela Royston.
      p. cm. -- (How can we save our world?)
  Includes bibliographical references and index.
  ISBN 978-1-84837-291-7 (hardcover : alk. paper)
  1. Renewable energy sources--Juvenile literature. 2. Energy
resources--Juvenile literature. I. Title.
  TJ808.3.R685 2010
  333.79'4--dc22
                              2009000619

Picture Credits
Corbis: 10 (Smithsonian Institution), 11 (Bettmann), 15 (Will & Deni McIntyre),
17 (Paul Souders), 20 (YONHAP/epa), 21 (Thierry Roge/Reuters), 22 (John
Carnemolla/Australian Picture Library), 23 (Dai Kurokawa/epa), 24 (Ryan Pyle),
25 (Du Huaju/Xinhua Press), 30 (Ryan Pyle), 37 (Arctic-Images);
EASI-Images: 7 (Rob Bowden), 8 (Rob Bowden), 13 (Adrian Cooper),
31 (Adrian Cooper), 35 (Chris Fairclough); Mary Evans Picture Library: 9;
Pelamis: 28; Science Photo Library: cover (Sinclair Stammers), 26 (Martin
Bond), 27 (Claus Lunau/Bonnier Publications), 34 (Martin Bond), 39 (Peter
Menzel), 40 (Martin Bond), 41 (Martin Bond), 42 (Pasquale Sorrentino),
43 (Volker Steger); Shutterstock: 18 (Kodda), 19 (Yuriy Chertok), 32 (Petr Nad),
33 (John Keith), 36 (Marko Heuver), 38 (Ulrich Mueller).

Artwork on pages 12 and 14 by Phipps Design

CONTENTS

Who Needs Energy?

We all need energy. We need it to light and heat our homes, schools, and places of work. Without energy in the form of electricity, we could not cook, watch television, or play computer games. Without energy in the form of fuel, we would not be able to travel by aircraft, train, bus, or car.

Most of our energy comes from fossil fuels, such as coal, oil, and natural gas. Electricity is produced from these fuels in power stations. Natural gas is also used for central heating and for cooking. Oil is refined and used as fuel in aircraft, cars, trucks, ships, and other vehicles. Oil is also made into a vast range of synthetic materials, including plastic, paint, and detergents.

Sustainable energy

During the daytime, we receive free energy from the sun, which gives us light and heat. The sun also powers the wind and produces the movement of waves in the ocean. Sunlight, wind, and waves can be used to generate electricity.

This book focuses on electricity and the way it is generated. Some sources of energy,

PERSPECTIVE

The world's biggest blackout

"I was waiting for the local train when the lights flickered. Then it went black. I found my way upstairs and onto the street. [She then ran the nine miles home.] That night was great. Everyone from the neighborhood was sitting outside and catching up. The kids were surprised when they looked up and actually saw stars—something that never happens in Manhattan."

On the *Engineering News Record*'s website, a New York City worker tells of her experiences on August 14, 2003, when a massive power outage occurred across the northeastern US and throughout Ontario, Canada, affecting 50 million people.

such as the wind and the waves, continue day after day. They are said to be renewable, or sustainable, sources of energy. Supplies of coal, gas, and some other sources of energy, however, are limited. One day these sources will run out, so they are described as non-renewable, or unsustainable.

Increasing demand

The demand for electricity has risen rapidly in recent decades. The standard of living in rich countries, such as the US and Japan, and in poorer countries, such as China and India, has risen. More people own computers and other electrical goods, and many buildings are air-conditioned. All these things use electricity. As the demand for electricity increases, the stocks of non-renewable resources shrink.

Like most cities, the Japanese capital, Tokyo, consumes huge amounts of energy. Electricity is used to light buildings and the streets. Less visible is the energy used for heat, air conditioning, and transportation.

FACE THE **FACTS**

This table shows the projected increase in world energy consumption between 2005 and 2030.

Year	Quadrillion Btu*
2005	462
2010	513
2015	563
2020	608
2025	652
2030	695

Btu = British thermal units

Source: Energy Information Administration (EIA), International Energy Outlook 2008

CHAPTER 1

From Candles to Lightbulbs

For thousands of years, people used sources of energy, such as wood, wind power, and sunlight, that were almost entirely sustainable. However, in the nineteenth century the Industrial Revolution introduced machinery that enabled people to access fossil fuels quickly and easily. Coal and oil were mined in increasing quantities.

This old Swedish windmill is no longer used but stands as a monument to the past.

Until the nineteenth century, people relied on animals for transportation, and burned mainly wood and other natural materials for heating and lighting. Candles were made from tallow (animal fat) or beeswax. Oil lamps, which burned olive oil or another plant oil, gave a brighter light than candles. The wind or running water was used to power machinery, for example, the wheels in mills that ground grain into flour.

Coal and steam

Coal had been used since ancient times—it gave more heat than wood and was used to smelt iron. After 1775, when James Watt invented an efficient steam engine, coal began to be mined in large quantities. The steam that powered Watt's engines came from water heated over burning coal. The first steam engines were used in Britain to pump out water that seeped into mines, but soon they were being used in factories and for pulling wagons along metal tracks. By the 1830s, railway carriages pulled by steam engines were carrying passengers between many British towns and cities.

The industrial age

The Industrial Revolution transformed the way in which goods were made and transported. Cheap goods were produced in factories and sold to people at home and abroad. The revolution spread from Britain to Europe, North America, and around the world, and it was driven by the move from sustainable energy to coal. The demand for coal increased dramatically.

This print of an early steam train evokes the excitement and opportunities that rail travel brought. Trains carried goods and passengers and were faster and cheaper than horse-drawn carriages and canal boats.

FACE THE **FACTS**

About 5,000 years ago, the energy people consumed for their survival came mainly from plants and animals and averaged about 12,000 kilocalories per person each day. As society became more advanced, the demand for energy slowly grew until, in AD 1400, each person was consuming about twice as much energy (26,000 kilocalories). Following the Industrial Revolution, the demand almost tripled to an average of 77,000 kilocalories per person in 1875. By 1975, it had more than tripled again to a staggering 230,000 kilocalories per person.

The discovery of electricity

In 1831, the British chemist and physicist Michael Faraday invented the first dynamo—a machine that could generate usable electricity. The electric telegraph and telephone were patented soon after. The most prolific inventor was Thomas Edison. He set up an inventions "factory" and filed patents for more than 1,000 inventions. One of them, in 1879, was for an electric lightbulb.

Electric lighting

Electric lighting was cleaner and safer than existing forms of light, which, by that time, included gaslights that burned gas made from coal. But before electric lighting could be used and charged for, Edison had to invent a light switch, an electric meter, and all the other equipment needed. Electricity supply companies were formed, and by 1890, several homes in New York, London, and elsewhere had switched to the new source of energy.

FACE THE **FACTS**

To invent an electric lightbulb, Thomas Edison had to find a substance that would glow white-hot but not burn up when electricity passed through it. Metal melted, so he tried carbonized paper, wood, fishing line, and many other substances. The bulb glowed but lasted no more than a few minutes. Then he tried cotton thread. He wrote, "It burned like an evening star for 45 hours, then the light went out with an appalling, unexpected suddenness."

This lightbulb was constructed in Thomas Edison's workshop in Menlo Park, New Jersey. It used bamboo for the filament and was the most successful lamp to be tested in his inventions factory. Today's incandescent lightbulbs work on the same principle as Edison's first bulbs.

Oil

In 1859, the first oil well was drilled in Pennsylvania. At first, oil was used in lamps for lighting, but after the invention of the gasoline engine by Karl Benz in the 1870s, it was also used to fuel cars, trucks, trains, and, eventually, aircraft. Demand for oil increased rapidly during the twentieth century as transportation became cheaper and more popular, and oil also came to be used in power stations to generate electricity. From 1950 on, the plastics industry expanded, producing a huge range of oil-based synthetic materials, such as rayon and polythene, and essential ingredients in medicines and other products.

Gas

Natural gas is a more efficient fuel than coal and oil, producing more heat and less pollution. It is found underground, usually alongside oil, and, until the 1970s, was often burned off at oil wells as a waste product. Today, it is piped to buildings to fuel stoves and central heating systems and is also used in gas-fired power stations.

The first commercial oil well, which was built by Edwin Drake in 1859, led to an oil boom in western Pennsylvania. Oil wells like these were sunk almost one on top of the other and led to oil spills, fires, and accidents.

11

Increasing demand

Throughout the twentieth century, demand for electricity increased. The earliest power stations were fueled either by coal or water. In countries with large supplies of coal, power stations were built close to the coalfields. The earliest hydropower station was built on the Fox River in Wisconsin in 1882. As demand grew, new kinds of power station were designed, fueled by oil and gas. In 1954, the world's first nuclear power station was opened in Obninsk, near Moscow, in Russia.

How a power station works

At a power station, electricity is produced in a generator, which works on the same principle as Michael Faraday's dynamo. A coil of wire is wound around a shaft, which is surrounded by a strong magnet. When the shaft revolves, it generates electricity in the wire. The shaft is turned by a turbine—but what turns the turbine?

In a hydroelectric power station, the force of moving water is used to turn the blades of the turbine. But in most large power stations, steam, produced by

Follow the arrows from the pile of coal through the power station to see how electricity is generated. From the transformer, the electricity is transmitted at high voltage.

Inside a coal-fired power station

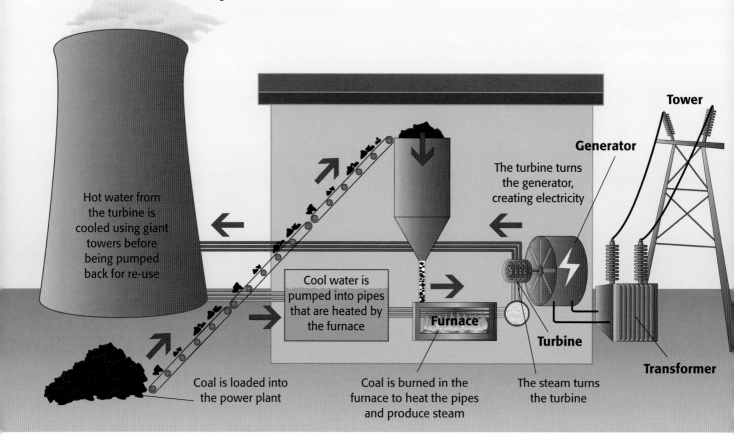

Hot water from the turbine is cooled using giant towers before being pumped back for re-use

The turbine turns the generator, creating electricity

Tower

Generator

Cool water is pumped into pipes that are heated by the furnace

Furnace

Turbine

Transformer

Coal is loaded into the power plant

Coal is burned in the furnace to heat the pipes and produce steam

The steam turns the turbine

burning coal, oil, or natural gas, is used to turn the turbine. Nuclear power stations, however, do not burn fuel but use heat produced by a nuclear reaction.

Distributing electricity

Electricity is carried from the power station through cables to homes, factories, businesses, and streets. The cables form a grid that is supplied with electricity from many different power stations. The electric current generated in the power station is many times stronger than the current that is needed. Before the current is fed into the grid, a transformer in the power station increases its strength, or voltage, even more. This is because electricity transmitted at high voltages is more energy efficient than electricity transmitted at lower voltages.

Substations

Thick, heavy power lines carry the high-voltage electricity to substations near towns and other places where it is needed. In the substation, the voltage is decreased to a level that is suitable for use. Thinner electric cables then distribute the electricity locally.

FACE THE **FACTS**

Coal-fired power stations produce more electricity than other kinds of power station (see table below).

Energy type	Percentage of world's electricity supply
Coal	39
Gas	19
Nuclear	17
Oil	16
Hydro	7
Others	2

Source: OECD/IEA World Energy Outlook 2004

Engineers work on an electricity tower in China. Strong poles are needed to carry the heavy cables high above the countryside. Electricity cables are lethal, so the engineers need to be very careful.

CHAPTER 2

Problems with Fossil Fuels

Three-quarters of the world's energy is generated by burning fossil fuels—coal, oil, and natural gas. Not only are fossil fuels unsustainable, they are contributing to global warming. This is a huge problem for the world.

Coal, oil, and natural gas are called fossil fuels because they formed millions of years ago from the fossilized remains of plants and tiny marine animals. When the plants and animals died, they were covered by silt and mud, which prevented them from rotting away completely. When living things rot, they produce carbon dioxide (CO_2). As the fossil fuels formed, however, their carbon was locked into them. Under pressure, the mud slowly turned to rock and the plant and animal remains changed into coal, oil, or natural gas.

Oil and gas form very slowly over millions of years. The oil is trapped between layers of rocks that are impermeable, which means they do not allow the oil to pass through them. To reach the oil, prospectors have to drill through these impermeable rocks.

How oil and gas formed

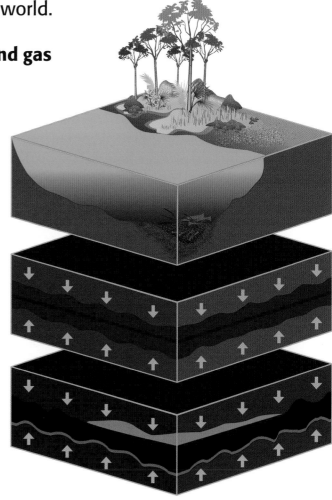

Remains of tiny plants and animals collected on the seabed.

Pressure produced by the layers of sediments and rock above changed the plant and animal remains into oil.

Layers of rock trapped oil, natural gas, and water.

Limited supplies

Fossil fuels are found in many different parts of the world, but there is a limited supply of them. They formed very slowly in particular circumstances and are not being replaced. The most abundant and easy to reach stocks of oil are running out fast, and in many countries reserves of coal, oil, and gas are in decline. More than half of all the world's stocks of oil have already been used. At the present rate of consumption, oil reserves will have dried up by 2050.

Pollution

Stocks of coal will last longer, but coal creates more pollution than oil or gas. Fossil fuels contain many different substances mixed together, and coal contains the most. Burning coal produces gases, such as sulfur dioxide and carbon dioxide, which escape into the atmosphere. When sulfur dioxide dissolves in rain, it forms a weak acid. This "acid rain" can kill trees and make lakes too acidic for fish and other animals to survive.

PERSPECTIVE

Past their peak

"There is simply not enough [oil and gas] to go around, and consumers will have to use less fuel. There are vast reserves of oil and gas, but we have used up the best stuff and what is left is slow and expensive to extract."

In the *Guardian* (a United Kingdom) newspaper in August 2008, a member of the British Institution of Gas Engineers gives a reason for the sudden rise in oil and gas prices.

The trees in this pine forest on Mount Mitchell in North Carolina have been badly damaged by acid rain.

Greenhouse gases

The biggest problem with burning fossil fuels is that it releases carbon dioxide into the atmosphere. The air also contains water vapor, methane, and other gases, which, along with carbon dioxide, are known as greenhouse gases. Greenhouse gases trap some of the sun's heat, making the earth warmer than it would otherwise be.

Without any greenhouse gases, the earth would be too cold to support the many species of life that survive here. However, people are adding so much carbon dioxide to the air each year that the average temperature at the earth's surface is getting warmer. This global warming means it could soon be too warm for many species of plant and animal to survive.

Climate change

Between 1750 and 2009, the average temperature of the earth warmed by less than 1.8 degrees Fahrenheit (°F)(1 degree Celcius °C), but already this small increase has caused huge disruption. The weather is now more unpredictable and extreme, and climates around the world are changing. Some areas are experiencing unusually long droughts, while others are hit by floods. Hurricanes are becoming more severe and frequent.

Scientists are extremely worried about the effects of climate change. The increase in temperature affects some parts of the world more than others. The Arctic, for example, has warmed up faster than most places and ice that used to be permanent is beginning to melt. If global warming continues, melting ice will cause sea levels to rise, flooding low-lying islands and coastal land.

Opposite: In summer, much of the land ice in the Arctic and Antarctic melts, pouring extra water into the sea. Even a small rise in sea levels will flood low-lying coasts.

SUSTAINABLE DEVELOPMENTS

Can fossil fuels be cleaned up?

Scientists are developing ways of preventing the CO_2 produced by burning coal from reaching the atmosphere. This is known as carbon capture and storage. We can trap and store up to 90 percent of the CO_2 emitted before it reaches the atmosphere. The first coal-fired power station to use carbon capture technology opened in Spremberg, Germany, in 2008. The problem is that carbon capture and storage is very expensive. Environmentalists say it is cheaper to build power stations that do not burn fossil fuels.

Change is urgent

The buildup of carbon dioxide in the atmosphere and the warming of the earth are both speeding up at an alarming rate. If people and governments allow this to continue, it could mean that in the future, it will be impossible to live in large parts of the world. Agriculture may fail and millions of people will be driven from their homes by famine as well as by rising sea levels. A quarter of the world's species are already threatened with extinction, partly because of climate change. People need to reduce drastically the amount of fossil fuels they burn. The generation of electricity accounts for 25 percent of all greenhouse gases produced by human beings.

Wasting energy

One way to reduce carbon emissions immediately is to cut out waste. About a third of the energy used in buildings is wasted. For example, many people leave lights burning in empty rooms, televisions and computers on standby, and cell phone chargers plugged in after the phone is charged. Cutting out waste not

Steam pours from the cooling towers of a power station. If all of this waste heat could be captured and re-used, the power station could burn less fuel.

only saves carbon emissions, it also saves money. Families could reduce heating costs by insulating their homes better. The insulation would also keep their rooms cooler in summer and so save on air conditioning.

Lost in transmission

Conventional power stations waste energy, too. For example, only about 25 percent of the energy available in coal-fired power stations reaches your home as electricity. About 60 percent is lost as waste heat in the power station. The rest is lost as the electricity is transmitted from the power station through the grid to your home. Combined heat and power (CHP) stations waste much less energy (see page 41).

As day dawns, many of the lights in this building are still burning. Office buildings are often lit all night, even though no one is in them.

FACE THE **FACTS**

Conventional lightbulbs work on the same principle as Edison's original lightbulb—they produce light by heating a filament until it is white-hot. This means that most of the electricity they use is wasted as heat. Compact fluorescent lightbulbs (CFLs), however, are low-energy bulbs. They create light by passing an electric current through certain types of gas. They use about 80 percent less electricity than a conventional bulb. They also last up to 12 times as long, so that fewer of them need to be manufactured.

CHAPTER 3

Nuclear Power

Since nuclear power stations do not burn fossil fuels, many people, including some scientists and politicians, claim that they are sustainable and emit no greenhouse gases. Most environmentalists, however, disagree. They say that nuclear power damages the environment at every stage of the process.

In 2008, nuclear power stations in 31 countries generated about 17 percent of the world's electricity. France relies most heavily on nuclear power and derives about 75 percent of its electricity from this source. The US has 104 nuclear power stations, which together supply about 20 percent of the country's electricity.

It takes many years and a huge amount of concrete to build a nuclear power station. Building new nuclear power stations is neither quick nor cheap.

Nuclear fission

All substances are made up of atoms. Each atom consists of electrons and a nucleus containing protons and neutrons. When an atom is split, it releases a huge amount of heat. So instead of burning fossil fuels, a nuclear power station uses a nuclear reaction to produce the heat needed to make steam to generate electricity.

Uranium is a substance whose atoms naturally split, or decay, very slowly over millions of years. In a power station, they are bombarded by neutrons, which split the atoms in less than a second. The splitting of one atom releases neutrons, which then bombard the surrounding atoms. Atomic bombs use this reaction to produce an uncontrolled explosion. In a power station, the reaction is controlled and the heat produced is used to make steam.

Members of the environmental group Greenpeace stage an anti-nuclear-power protest outside the headquarters of a Dutch political party.

Danger of radiation

The breaking up of atoms gives off radioactive rays and particles. As radioactive substances decay, they produce radiation, which damages—and can kill—living things. The nuclear reaction is therefore dangerous and has to be contained within the power station. Thick layers of concrete surround the reactor and the whole structure. Nevertheless, accidents still happen. On April 26, 1986, for example, the world's worst nuclear accident occurred at the Chernobyl nuclear power station in Ukraine. The reactor caught fire and created a deadly cloud of radioactivity that traveled around the world.

PERSPECTIVE

Nuclear power— no thanks!

"Despite what the nuclear industry tells us, building enough nuclear power stations to make a meaningful reduction in greenhouse gas emissions would cost trillions of dollars, create tens of thousands of tons of lethal high-level radioactive waste, and result in a Chernobyl-scale accident once every decade."

The environmental organization Greenpeace

Radioactive waste

Nuclear power stations produce radioactive waste, which remains dangerous for at least a thousand years. It has to be safely stored and monitored to make sure radiation does not escape into the environment. This costs billions of dollars, and the problem is increasing: each nuclear power station produces on average 22 tons (20 metric tons) of radioactive waste a year. No one has yet found a way to dispose of this waste safely.

Mining uranium

Although nuclear power stations do not produce greenhouse gases, mining and preparing uranium does. Uranium is widely but thinly spread throughout many rocks, which means that huge quantities of rocks have to be mined and processed to produce the uranium rods used in a nuclear reactor.

Uranium mines ravage the countryside and pollute nearby rivers and lakes with radioactive waste. Canada is the world's leading producer of uranium, mining about 25 percent of the total amount used each year.

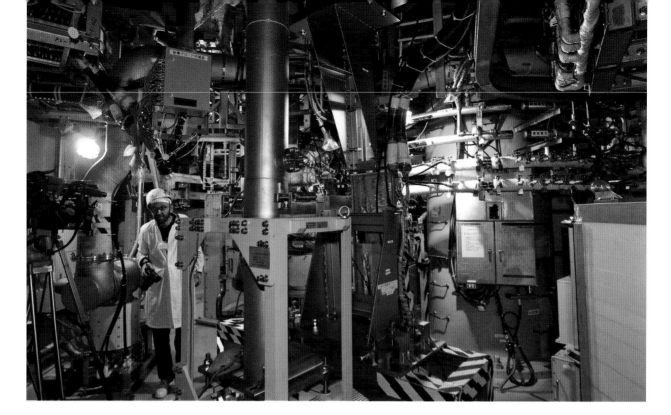

Nuclear fusion

Scientists are working on an alternative type of nuclear power. Instead of splitting atoms in nuclear fission, they combine them in nuclear fusion. When two atoms of hydrogen are combined—fused—to produce one atom of helium, they release a huge amount of energy. The energy of the sun is produced by nuclear fusion.

Scientists have already built small, experimental nuclear fusion reactors. So far, they have produced only small amounts of energy, but even this is a remarkable achievement given the scientific obstacles they have had to overcome. Although the reaction itself is simple, it occurs only at extremely high temperatures or if the atoms are crashed together at very high speed. The existing models have used temperatures much hotter than those at the center of the sun.

The benefits

If nuclear fusion can be made to work on a large scale, it will bring huge benefits. Only small amounts of fuel are needed to produce large amounts of energy, and both the fuel and the waste produced are much less radioactive than that produced by nuclear fission. However, the most optimistic scientists admit that a working fusion power station is at least 40 to 50 years away. Some scientists doubt that it is possible at all.

This research laboratory, called JT60, is run by the Japan Atomic Energy Association. Scientists from many countries are working together on nuclear fusion.

FACE THE **FACTS**

In 1989, two scientists claimed that they had achieved nuclear fusion at room temperature. If this were possible, it could give a cheap and available source of clean energy. Scientists around the world were very excited, and many tried to repeat the experiments. Unfortunately, none have yet succeeded.

CHAPTER 4

Water and Wind Power

The force of moving water and the force of the wind are sustainable sources of energy. They are natural forces that can be harnessed to generate electricity in several different ways. Also, once the facilities for generating water and wind power have been built, they produce no greenhouse gases in the process of generating electricity.

Electricity produced by moving water is called hydroelectricity. Tides, currents, and the wind cause the sea to move constantly, but the greatest source of hydroelectricity is rivers. Streams and rivers flow from high ground to lower ground and into lakes or the sea. Rivers were used to generate electricity as long ago as 1882, but people soon discovered that by building a dam across a river and allowing water to flow through it under great pressure, they could produce a stronger force and, therefore, more electricity. The flowing water turns a turbine, which turns a generator.

The easiest place to dam a river is where it flows through a narrow valley between mountains or hills. So it is not surprising that mountainous countries, such as Norway and Vietnam, rely most on hydroelectricity. Norway produces almost all of its electricity from hydropower. Canada generates more hydroelectricity than any other country, although it supplies only two-thirds of its needs.

A dam wall has to be strong enough to hold back billions of gallons of water and to resist earthquakes. Floods caused by a dam bursting are very rare.

The Thre Gorges Dam in China is the largest hydroelectric power station in the world. It has been built across the Yangtze River, creating a reservoir that is about 410 miles long (660 kilometers). The dam wall is 101 meters high (330 feet) and about 1.2 miles long (2 km).

PERSPECTIVE

Three Gorges Dam protest

"Many people have no place to stay now. We have to stay at relatives' places. The compensation is not what we expected. It is not enough. One local resident was so upset, she jumped into the water and was rescued by government officials."

A resident from the last village to be cleared for the building of China's Three Gorges Dam, quoted on the news website Terra Daily. Three Gorges is the largest dam in the world—1.4 million people were displaced during its construction.

The disadvantages of hydropower

Operating a hydroelectric power station produces almost no greenhouse gases, but building a power station has a huge effect on the environment. The dam wall is constructed of thick concrete, whose manufacture produces carbon dioxide. The largest dams flood vast areas of land. The people living there are forced to move for the dam to be built. People who live below a dam are affected too. The river, which may have been used to irrigate farmland, is reduced to a trickle, while river animals and plants lose their habitat.

Tidal barrages

Dams—or barrages—can also harness the power of the tide. The level of the sea is constantly rising and falling, giving two high tides and two low tides every day. In some places, such as large river estuaries, the changing tide creates a fast current of water. The first tidal power station was built across La Rance estuary in France in 1966. As the rising tide pushes water through the barrage, it turns the turbine to generate electricity. As the tide falls, the water is held behind the barrage and then released to turn the turbine in the opposite direction.

La Rance tidal power station generates 70 megawatts of electricity a year, enough for a city of about 300,000 people. The electricity generated is cheaper than from any other source in France.

The disadvantages of tidal barrages

The flow of the tide is renewable energy, and once built, tidal power stations produce almost no carbon dioxide. Ecologists, however, usually oppose the building of a tidal barrage because it changes the environment on both sides of the barrier, threatening the habitats of wetland birds and other wildlife. Like dams across rivers, tidal barrages are expensive to build. However, there is now a new way of exploiting tidal power—tidal turbines.

Under the sea

A tidal turbine is fixed to the seabed in the path of a strong tidal current. The water turns the blades that power the generator. Several turbines can be constructed close together, creating a tidal "farm". The first commercial tidal turbine, constructed in Strangford Lough in Northern Ireland, UK, began generating electricity in 2008.

Tidal generators are much cheaper to build than tidal barrages, and there are more places around the coast where they will work well. Tidal turbines are similar to wind turbines (see page 29), but they are more reliable and therefore more efficient. Unlike the force of the wind, the force of the tide is predictable and unfailing.

Only a small part of the tidal turbine shows above the ocean surface. The blades that turn the turbine are hidden under the sea. They are fixed to a strong tower that is sunk firmly into the seabed.

SUSTAINABLE DEVELOPMENTS

Tidal power sites

Tidal turbines are best sited in places with strong tidal currents, such as river estuaries and narrow channels between landmasses. Places that have been pinpointed as good sites for tidal power include Bass Strait, Australia; Bay of Fundy, Canada; Golden Gate, San Francisco Bay, US; Pentland Firth, Scotland; Morecambe Bay, England; Strait of Gibraltar (between Spain and Morocco); Strait of Malacca (between Singapore and Indonesia); and Wando Hoenggan waterway, South Korea.

Wave power

Tides are not the only force moving the sea. Waves, whipped up by winds, travel across the surface. You can see their power when they crash onto the shore. About 60 percent of the world's population lives within 40 miles (64 km) of the coast, putting them within reach of electricity generated by wave power.

A Pelamis machine harnesses wave power to generate electricity. The name Pelamis means "sea snake".

Scientists and inventors are devising different ways of tapping the energy in waves. The most developed is Pelamis, an anchored, jointed device that bobs on the surface. The movement at the joints is transformed into a force that drives the generator. The electricity is fed into the grid through cables on the seabed. The first large wave-power station was begun in 2008 off the coast of Portugal. Three wave machines already provide power for about 1,500 homes, but 25 more machines are planned.

The disadvantages of wave power

One of the main problems with wave power is that waves vary with the strength of the wind. This means that strong winds and rough seas will provide lots of energy, while light winds and calm seas will provide almost no energy. Wave machines are situated where there is usually enough wind to power them. Nevertheless, they have to be strong enough—and anchored securely enough—to withstand the severest gales.

Wind power

A wind turbine works in the same way as a tidal turbine (see page 27), except that the turbine is powered by moving air—the wind—instead of moving water. Wind is a renewable and sustainable source of energy, and once built, the turbines produce no carbon dioxide. Less greenhouses gas is produced in the manufacture of the turbines than is emitted in the building of conventional power stations.

In many countries, wind turbines are the most common and visible form of sustainable energy. They range from small turbines on individual buildings to large turbines in the countryside or, largest of all, offshore or in a lake. When many large turbines are erected close together, they are called a wind farm.

FACE THE **FACTS**

Local people sometimes object to the erection of new wind farms. For example, the British government wanted to construct 181 turbines on the Scottish island of Lewis. Local people were worried about spoiling the land on which the turbines were to be built. They warned that many archaeological sites and the habitats of rare birds, such as golden eagles and merlin, could be damaged.

Onshore wind farms

Many countries are investing in wind farms. The US has the most wind farms and plans to build several more. It is best to erect wind turbines on hilltops and open plains, where there is a steady wind most of the year. The Maranchon wind farm, for example, one of the biggest wind farms, is situated on the Spanish plain, northeast of Madrid. Coasts tend to be windy, so many wind farms are built on hilly ridges near the coast.

Offshore wind farms

However, offshore wind farms, built just off the coast or near the shores of lakes, have many advantages over those erected on land. The turbines are more expensive than land-based ones because they are bigger. However, these turbines generate more electricity, and because they are out of sight, local people are less likely to object to them. Britain is planning a huge wind farm called the London Array in the estuary of the Thames River. It will have up to 341 turbines and should eventually provide electricity for up to 750,000 Londoners.

This factory in Urumqi, China, manufactures wind turbines. Wind turbines are enormous; the largest is more than 330 feet tall (100 meters). The larger the turbines, the fewer are needed in a wind farm.

This huge wind farm in the Mojave Desert supplies electricity to the residents of Los Angeles, California. The city plans to generate a fifth of its electricity from renewable sources by 2010.

The disadvantages of wind farms

The main disadvantage of wind turbines is that they only work when the wind is blowing between 7 and 53 miles per hour (mph) (11 and 86 kilometers per hour, kph). The turbine turns to face the direction of the wind, but if the wind exceeds 53 mph (86 kph) per hour, it has to close down. Small turbines for individual buildings are only useful in very windy places. In most large towns and cities, there are not enough windy days to make them worthwhile. It has been calculated that in many cities, the CO_2 produced in manufacturing a small wind turbine is greater than the amount that would be saved by using the turbine.

SUSTAINABLE DEVELOPMENTS

Powered by kites

Scientists at Delft University in the Netherlands have pioneered a wind turbine powered by kites! The generator on the ground is turned by several massive kites tethered to it. The kites fly 2,625 feet above the ground (800 m), where the wind is stronger. Makani, an American-based kite company, is working on a similar project. An Italian kite company claims that a turbine powered by four 600-square-yard (500-square-meter) kites could produce as much electricity as an average coal-fired power station.

CHAPTER 5

Solar Power

Every minute, the sun beams enough energy onto the earth to satisfy our energy needs for a year. The problem is that solar energy is spread thinly across the earth's surface, so that most of it is wasted. The challenge for scientists is to collect and concentrate enough solar energy to generate electricity.

Solar energy will last as long as the sun shines and is a renewable source, at least for the next 10 billion years! There are two main ways that the sun's energy can be used to generate electricity. The first uses photovoltaic (PV) cells to collect sunlight and transform it into electricity. With the second method, large solar power stations use mirrors to concentrate the sun's heat to produce steam to turn a turbine.

Best sites

The sun's energy varies throughout the day and is not spread evenly across the world. It is strongest in the tropics on either side of the equator, where the sun beams down directly. The best places to take advantage of solar energy are the sunburned deserts north and south of the equator, but it can be harnessed in cooler, cloudier places too.

In cooler climates, photovoltaic cells are mounted at an angle so that the midday sun shines directly onto them.

Photovoltaic cells

Photovoltaic cells contain a substance, such as silicon, that generates electricity when light falls on it. These cells are attached as tiles to the roof of a building, where they generate electricity for lighting and machines such as computers. However, they have to be placed on roofs that face the sun at midday, when the sunlight is strongest, and, of course, they do not work at night. Nevertheless, even in cooler countries photovoltaic cells can work so well in summer that they generate more electricity than is needed. In some countries, such as Germany, electricity companies buy back the extra electricity and feed it into the national grid.

Photovoltaic cells being laid right onto a roof. In tropical countries, where the sun is mainly overhead, the cells can be laid flat. To work efficiently, they have to be cleaned regularly.

FACE THE **FACTS**

One way to collect solar power 24 hours a day is to have a satellite that collects solar energy and beams it down as microwaves to antennae on earth. At first, this seems like a good idea, but the satellite would need huge groups of solar cells several miles long. The cost of getting them into space and assembling them there makes the project far more expensive than ground-based alternatives.

This vast array of PV cells is generating electricity for a photovoltaic power station. The panels cover a large area of ground and so are best situated in deserts or on land that is not otherwise needed.

Cheaper alternative

Photovoltaic cells for roofs are expensive, but a thinner, cheaper alternative is being developed for windows. The glass panes are covered with a transparent film that collects the sunlight and feeds it to cells in the window frame. Thinner, cheaper cells that are printed on aluminum foil are also being developed for solar power stations.

Photovoltaic power stations

Some solar power stations use photovoltaic cells. For example, the Nellis Solar Power station in Nevada, which took less than a year to build, is the largest photovoltaic power station in the US. It has 70,000 groups of PV cells and generates electricity for the airbase in which it is located.

A much larger photovoltaic power station is planned in the Australian state of Victoria. At this station, sunlight will be collected by mirrors and focused onto the photovoltaic cells, making the cells 1,500 times more powerful than ordinary solar panels. When the station is completed in 2013, it will supply electricity to 45,000 homes.

Concentrated solar power

A different type of concentrated solar power station uses mirrors to concentrate the sun's heat. The heat, which can reach 1,049°F (565°C), is used to produce steam to power a turbine and generator, as in a conventional power station. Since solar power stations cannot work at night, some of the heat they produce during the day is stored. In addition, they often work alongside gas-fired power stations, which can generate electricity after dark.

Future possibilities

Scientists calculate that covering just 5 percent of the hottest deserts with solar power stations could eventually produce enough electricity for the whole world. European countries are already considering a plan to build a string of solar power stations under the intense sun of the Sahara Desert.

PERSPECTIVE

Exploiting the desert sun

"We don't make enough use of deserts. The sun beats down on them mercilessly during the day and heats the ground to tremendous temperatures. Then at night that heat is radiated back into the atmosphere. It is completely wasted. We need to exploit the vast amounts of energy that the sun beams down on us."

A scientist involved in a scheme to build solar power stations in the Sahara Desert, quoted in the *Guardian* newspaper.

Mirrors reflect the sun's rays onto a central tower, producing enough heat to power this concentrated solar power station.

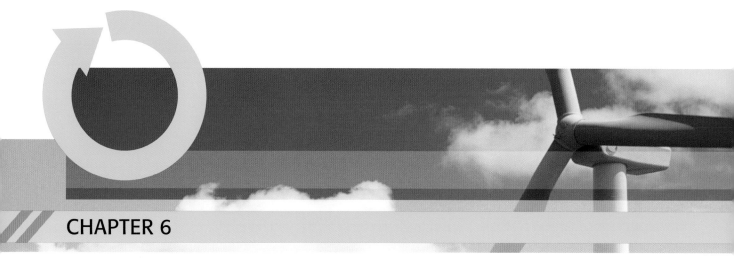

CHAPTER 6

Other Sources of Power

Scientists are developing new and better ways of producing electricity from sustainable sources of energy. Solar power, wind power, and hydropower are becoming cheaper and more effective, but they are not the only sources of sustainable energy. Others include geothermal power and biomass.

When water meets with hot rocks 6,560 feet (2,000 m) below the earth's surface, it boils and erupts in a geyser.

Geothermal energy is heat that comes from the earth itself. The center of the earth is blazing hot, and in places, molten volcanic rock spills onto the surface. Geysers are springs of steaming water that has been heated deep underground.

Geothermal power stations

Geothermal power stations use the earth's own heat to produce steam to drive turbines and generate electricity. Iceland, which has several active volcanoes, already produces about a fifth of its electricity from geothermal energy. In addition, hot water from geysers is used to centrally heat 87 percent of Icelandic homes. The first geothermal power stations were built in Italy and New Zealand more than 50 years ago, but today several countries, including Japan and the US, generate some geothermal electricity.

This geothermal power station in Iceland produces 76.5 megawatts of electricity and about 124 gallons (475 liters) of hot water each second. Surplus water from the plant is used to supply a vacation resort nearby.

Heat pumps

Geothermal heat is used in another way to heat and cool individual buildings. In nearly all of the places where people live, the ground just a few yards below the surface is at a constant temperature of between 44.6 and 68°F (7 and 20°C) . A heat pump uses the difference in temperature between the earth's surface and underground to move heat in or out of a building. In cold weather, liquid from the surface is pumped through the warmer rocks below to heat it and is then piped into the building. In summer, the reverse happens. The rocks belowground are colder than the rocks near the surface, so warm water from the building is pumped through the colder rocks to cool it. The cool liquid then circulates through the building.

Hot Earth

The rocks below our feet are hot because they contain radioactive substances that produce heat as they slowly decay. In addition, rocks near the surface take in and store some heat from the sun. Natural radioactivity and solar heat are both continuing and sustainable. Geothermal energy can be used day and night and all year round, and although it takes advantage of radioactivity, it does not produce radioactive waste.

Biomass

Biomass is fuel that is produced by living things. For example, wood and agricultural waste, such as straw, can be burned to produce energy. Biomass also includes animal and human waste, which, with the help of bacteria, can be turned into methane, or natural gas.

Biomass is sustainable because living things can easily be renewed. It is said to be carbon neutral because it neither adds to nor reduces the amount of extra carbon dioxide in the air. Green plants take in carbon dioxide from the air and through the process of photosynthesis make sugar, starch, and cellulose, which the plants use to grow. Plants, therefore, become a temporary store of carbon. When they rot or are burned, the carbon stored in them returns to the air as the gas carbon dioxide.

This biofuel power station in Germany burns wood to make electricity. Burning wood is less efficient than burning fossil fuels, but this does not matter if the power station is a combined heat and power plant that captures waste heat and uses it to heat nearby buildings.

FACE THE **FACTS**

Biomass stoves and power stations are carbon neutral only when the fuel they burn comes from local sources. For example, Britain is planning to build several large biomass power stations that will burn wood and agricultural waste shipped in from around the world. They will not be truly carbon neutral because ships burn fossil fuels, creating extra greenhouse gases.

Solid fuel

Wood has long been burned to produce heat, but in open fires much of the heat escapes up the chimney. Wood-burning stoves are more efficient and can burn wood chips or logs as a direct source of heat or to heat water. Biomass is also used instead of fossil fuels in some power stations. Wood and other plant remains do not produce as much heat as fossil fuels, however, and biomass power stations work best when they are kept small and used as part of a combined heat and power station (see page 40).

Making methane

As a greenhouse gas, methane is 21 times as powerful as carbon dioxide in trapping the sun's heat. Living things produce methane, especially when they rot. As bacteria break down sewage and as waste food and other organic materials rot in landfill sites, methane escapes into the air. However, methane is a good fuel and is the main ingredient in natural gas. Some landfill sites and sewage farms now collect methane to use in fuel cells (see page 42) to generate electricity.

This farmer in Gujarat, India, uses cow dung to make methane gas. He mixes the dung with water before pouring it into the main, covered tank. In just a few hours, the tank produces enough methane to power a cooking stove.

CHAPTER 7

Saving Energy

In addition to switching to sustainable sources of energy, we need to reduce the amount of energy we use. Huge amounts of energy are wasted at the power station, in the national grid, and in the way we use electricity.

About 60 percent of the energy is lost as waste heat that escapes as steam through cooling towers. Another 15 percent leaks away as the electricity is transmitted long distances through the grid (see page 13). Combined heat and power (CHP) stations reduce waste in two ways. They supply electricity to local buildings so that much less energy is lost in transmission. And they use the waste heat from generating electricity to heat water for local buildings. The water is used for central heating or as hot water for baths and other uses.

These pipes are being laid to carry hot water from a new extension to a combined heat and power scheme in Sheffield, UK.

The advantages of being small

Combined heat and power (CHP) stations are smaller than traditional power stations. They are often built to supply electricity to industrial complexes (which use a large amount of electricity) and to residential communities. They are so small, that residents do not even know they are there. Southampton, in the UK, has a CHP station in the middle of the city center.

The European company Solar Fabrik AG manufactures solar panels. The company uses its own panels on the front of the factory and on the roof to make electricity to power the plant. Excess electricity is sold back to the grid.

Many CHP stations are fueled by natural gas, but some are fueled by biomass. Biomass works well in a CHP station because the fuel can be sourced locally. These stations can also use a variety of fuels without having to alter their equipment, which means they can easily change from burning fossil fuel to burning straw and other agricultural waste as appropriate. For example, instead of burning sugar waste, which produces harmful pollution, the waste cane can be burned to generate electricity and heat.

FACE THE **FACTS**

Helsinki, the capital city of Finland, generates 90 percent of its electricity in CHP stations. In Denmark, 50 percent of the country's electricity is generated in CHP stations.

More efficient boilers

In addition to developing more efficient ways of generating electricity, scientists and engineers are designing better boilers for heating water and for central heating. Modern domestic boilers get more energy from the fuel they burn by capturing the heat in the exhaust fumes before it escapes into the air. The most efficient type of boiler is a combination boiler. Instead of heating a large tank of water for the hot water system, it only heats the water when the hot tap is turned on.

Fuel cells

Fuel cells are even more efficient than condensing boilers. Instead of fuel being burned to make heat, the heat is broken down to give a supply of hydrogen. The fuel cell combines hydrogen with oxygen from the air and the process generates electricity. Fuel cells are silent and the only waste they produce is heat and water. The heat can be used to warm water for central heating and a hot water supply.

This fuel cell, on the middle shelf, combines hydrogen and oxygen (from the air) to create electricity, heat, and water as a by-product. Fuel cells are clean and are up to three times more efficient than burning fuel to generate electricity. They usually work alongside a "fuel reformer", which extracts hydrogen from other fuels.

This CD player gets its power from a direct methanol fuel cell (DMFC) instead of from batteries. This kind of fuel cell uses methanol to make electricity without the methanol having to be changed into hydrogen first. A DMFC can make enough electricity to power a laptop but produces some carbon dioxide as waste.

Fuel cells have a wide range of uses. They have already been installed in some schools, hospitals, offices, and other large buildings. Any extra electricity they generate is sold back to the grid, so in addition to saving money, they can make money. Some cities have buses that run on fuel cells, and the cells are being adapted for use in cars, scooters, small boats, and other forms of transportation. The main disadvantage is their cost, but as the technology is developed, they should become cheaper.

SUSTAINABLE
DEVELOPMENTS

Micropower

Fuel cells can take the place of batteries in cell phones, laptop computers, and other devices. At the moment, these cells run on fuels such as methanol, but in the future, they are likely to run on water. To recharge your battery, all you will have to do is top it off with water.

Saving energy

Making power stations, domestic boilers, and electrical goods more efficient will all be useless unless consumers cut out waste too. Electricity is wasted in many small ways that you might think do not matter, such as leaving phone chargers plugged in after the battery is charged. We all need to improve the way we use energy and look for sustainable energy alternatives wherever possible.

biomass Plants and products of other living things that can be used as fuel.

carbon dioxide A gas that consists of carbon and oxygen combined. It is the most abundant damaging greenhouse gas produced by people.

combined heat and power (CHP) A power station that uses the waste heat produced by generating electricity to supply hot water to local buildings.

compact fluorescent lightbulb An energy-saving lightbulb that produces light when electricity is passed through a gas, making it glow.

condensing boiler A boiler that contains a device that condenses water vapor in the waste gases and recycles its heat.

extinction Wiping out altogether. A species of animal becomes extinct when there are no members of the species left alive.

filament A thin wire in a traditional lightbulb that becomes white-hot.

fossil fuels Fuels made from the remains of plants and marine animals that lived millions of years ago. Coal, oil, and natural gas are fossil fuels.

fuel cell A device that generates electricity by combining hydrogen and oxygen in a chemical reaction.

generator A machine linked to a turbine that spins to produce electricity.

geothermal Produced by the earth's internal heat.

geyser A spring of water that has been heated geothermally.

global warming An increase in the average temperature of the air at the surface of the earth.

greenhouse gases Gases in the atmosphere that trap the sun's heat.

hydroelectric Related to electricity produced by moving water.

incandescent Giving out light as a result of being heated to a high temperature.

Industrial Revolution A period in British history between about 1750 and 1850 when industry increased and goods began to be made in factories.

insulating Using a layer of material to keep heat from leaking out or in.

kilocalorie A measure of energy. It is the amount of heat needed to raise the temperature of 1 kilogram of water by 1°C.

landfill site A large hole in the ground in which garbage is buried.

methane A greenhouse gas that traps 21 times as much heat as carbon dioxide weight for weight. It is an efficient fuel and is the main constituent of natural gas.

microwaves High-frequency electromagnetic waves. They are used in microwave ovens and cell phones.

nuclear fission Splitting the nucleus of an atom to generate a large amount of energy, including heat.

nuclear fusion Combining the nuclei of two atoms of hydrogen to make helium, thereby releasing a large amount of energy.

nuclear reaction A reaction that changes the nucleus of an atom.

patent A government license to an inventor giving him or her sole right to make, use, or sell an invention for a limited period.

photosynthesis The process by which green plants make sugar by using the energy of sunlight to combine water and carbon dioxide.

photovoltaic (PV) cell A device that changes sunlight into electricity.

radiation Harmful rays or particles produced by a radioactive substance.

radioactive Giving off harmful rays because of the breaking up of atoms.

reactor A machine for splitting atoms to produce energy.

smelt To produce metal from ore by heating the ore until it melts.

species A particular kind of living thing. Only members of the same species can breed with one another.

substation Part of the electric grid where the voltage of the electric current is raised or lowered by transformers.

sulfur dioxide Gas that consists of sulfur and oxygen combined. Sulfur dioxide pollutes the air and causes acid rain.

synthetic Artificially made, usually from oil.

transformer A device that changes the voltage of a current of electricity.

turbine A wheel made of tightly packed metal blades, used to turn generators to produce electricity.

uranium A substance that is found in the ground. Uranium is radioactive because its atoms decay or split naturally.

voltage A measure of the strength of an electric force.

BOOKS

Bowden, Rob. *Sustainable World: Energy.* KidHaven Press, 2004.

Brown, Paul. *Sustainable Future: Energy and Resources.* Franklin Watts, 2000.

Chapman, Stephen. *Energy Essentials: Renewable Energy.* Raintree, 2005.

Royston, Angela. *Eco-Action: Energy of the Future.* Heinemann Library, 2007.

Smith, Trevor. *Renewable Energy Resources* Smart Apple Media, 2004.

Stringer, John. *Sustainable Futures: Energy.* Smart Apple Media, 2006.

Woodward, John. *Eyewitness: Climate Change.* Dorling Kindersley, 2008.

WEBSITES

www.ase.org/section/_audience/ consumers
Lots of tips for how to save electricity.

www.energysavingtrust.org.uk
How homes can be improved to save energy and how they can generate their own electricity.

www.epa.gov/climatechange/
United States Environmental Protection Agency's website on climate change.

www.fuelcells.org/?gclid=CJLix4fs_JYCFQ_UlAodX HU8YA
A site explaining how fuel cells work and the many ways they can be used.

home.clara.net/darvill/altenerg/tidal.htm
A website that explains how tidal power works and describes other forms of sustainable energy.

INDEX

Page numbers in **BOLD** refer to illustrations.